201 Writing Prompts

TO SPARK YOUR CREATIVITY & END WRITER'S BLOCK

Heather Wright

Saugeen Publishers

Canada

Heather Wright
wright_writer@hotmail.com

Book Layout ©2013 BookDesignTemplates.com

Ordering Information:

Quantity sales. Special discounts are available on quantity purchases by corporations, associations, and others. For details, contact the "Special Sales Department" at the address above.

201 Writing Prompts/ Heather Wright. —1st ed.
ISBN-13: 978-1500131630
ISBN-10: 1500131636

Contents

By Way of Introduction 7

Prompts 1 to 10 9

Prompts 11 to 20 13

Prompts 21 to 30 17

Prompts 31 to 40 21

Prompts 41 to 50 25

Prompts 51 to 60 29

Prompts 61 to 70 31

Prompts 71 to 80 33

Prompts 81 to 90 35

Prompts 91 to 100 39

Prompts 101 to 110 43

Prompts 111 to 120 47

Prompts 121 to 130 49

Prompts 131 to 140 53

Prompts 141 to 150 55

Prompts 151 to 160 57

Prompts 161 to 170 59

Prompts 171 to 180 61

Prompts 181 to 190 63

Prompts 191 to 201 65

Keeping the Writer in You Motivated 67

Final Words.. 71

Writing is the only thing that, when I do it, I don't feel I should be doing something else.

—*Gloria Steinem*

CHAPTER 1

By Way of Introduction

All writers have *those* days when inspiration just seems to fly out the window—when the blank screen becomes a sadly accurate reflection of the sorry state of your imagination and you start your fourth game of FreeCell in ten minutes. Or you have a day when the current writing project just sits there like an ugly pile of February slush—all memories of the lovely white snow it started out as are gone, and all it's good for is creeping in that one small hole in your boots and making your life miserable, wet and cold.

Some people call this writer's block. I call it a temporary pause in the creative process—I call it a lot of other things, too, but I'd have to change the rating on this book if I printed them.

The writing prompts in this book are for *those* days.

But they're also for the days when you just want to play with words. They're for those times when you need to clear your brain of the messiness of your day and warm up before tackling the project that means so much to you. They can serve as prompts for your daily writing journal, too. Trust me, if you break them down into their individual components, you'll have enough to last a year! Maybe you could share one with your writers' group one night and enjoy the completely different stories that emerge from the same prompt.

How you use the prompts is up to you, but I encourage you to use them for whatever purpose works for where your writing is right now.

The book is divided into chapters of ten random writing prompts each. The prompts come in a variety of formats from lists of titles and opening lines, to reflective questions, to random snatches of dialogue and brainstorming topics. Work through them in order, or dip into the book anywhere you please.

I hope you enjoy exploring these writing prompts, and I wish you many, many hours of imagination and creativity.

CHAPTER 2

Prompts 1 to 10

1. What's your favorite natural sound? Wind shaking poplar leaves? Ocean surf? Thunderstorms? One bird's song? Describe the place that the sound reminds you of. What other senses do you recall? Do you remember a special smell, taste, touch or sight associated with this place?

2. What do you need to have the best start to your day? Eight hours sleep? Two cups of coffee? Skipping morning altogether? Music? All news radio? What happens when your favorite morning routine goes wrong? Now answer these questions for your character.

3. Free write around one, some or all of the following words: toy, cup, tremble, weight, park

4. Begin a story or a poem with one of the following titles: Just a Dollar, Death Takes a Credit Card, Love Factually, Gone with the Sinned, Band, Snap Shot.

5. Use these bare bones of dialogue to create a scene between two people. Add setting, character, action and emotion to fill in the gaps.

I'm so glad you made it.

How many people did you tell?

Why?

I was followed. I'm asking you again. How many people did you tell?

Just Terry. Just one.

One too many.

6. In Stuart Kaminsky's Toby Peters mysteries, Toby has recurring nightmares that feature Bozo the clown. Write about your recurring dream or create one for your character.

7. If your characters live in the present, what photos or images do your characters have on their desktops or cell phone screens? Why is this image important? If your characters live in another time, what photos would they keep in a wallet or on a bedside table, or what poster would they have on their bedroom walls? Explain why certain photos or images are special to you?

8. What does your character consider a luxury? A day at the spa? Box tickets for a game? Feeling safe? A snow day home from school? One more day? What obstacles keep your character from enjoying this luxury? Describe what you would consider a luxury. If it is something that you can treat yourself to once in a while, how does it make you feel? If it is something that is out of reach, how important is it that you eventually get to enjoy it?

9. Freewrite around one, some or all of the following words: watch, car, bowl, sidewalk, apple

10. Use the following dialogue as a springboard to your story:

I brought it, as you asked.
Thank you.
Thank you? That's not much of a response considering ...
Considering what?
Considering the cost.

CHAPTER 3

Prompts 11 to 20

11. Use a song title as a title for your next story or poem. Consider Over the Rainbow, Unforgettable, No More Mr. Nice Guy, Taking a Chance on Love, Invincible.

12. Get away from the keyboard and write with pencil/pen and paper. This is the way you first started to create. The connections are still there. If you already write in longhand, change your paper, use colored pens, or change your location.

13. Think of a story that might go with one of these possible opening sentences:

- Mondays never go well.
- How can someone get lost twice in one day?
- Is that a threat?
- I definitely didn't like the way those lights were flickering?
- So young.

14. Use these bare bones of dialogue to create a scene between two people. Add setting, character, action, emotion to fill in the gaps.

The sun's almost down. Won't be long now.
Why do we have to wait until it's dark?
Ask him when he gets here.
Are you ready?
Are you?

15. Free write around one, some or all of the following: running, wondering, hiding, challenging, threatening

16. What makes your character impatient or angry? How does he or she deal with anger? Does your character keep it bottled up to explode later over something insignificant? Let it all out right at the moment and then move on? Never really get angry? Count to 10? React with fists or words? What does it take to get a strong reaction from your character? Think about how you handle anger. How does it affect you and your relationships?

17. What story might precede one of these closing lines? Maybe they could be used as opening lines, too.

- I had nothing left but thanks.
- Sunsets will never be the same again
- Kisses are just the beginning.
- Yup. Typical Michael.
- Home.

18. Do holiday festivals make you happy, or do they bring back sad memories, or do they do both? How do you deal with your holiday feelings? How do holidays affect your character?

19. Think about makes you laugh. Do you have a favorite comedian or TV show or movie? What makes the person or program so funny? What kind of humor appeals to you? Witty repartee? Slapstick? Farce? What makes your character laugh? One of the key rules of humor is, "Pain is funny." Do you think it's true? Why or why not?

20. Use one, some or all of the following words to create a story, poem or scene: ribbon, glass, silver, roof, pace.

Prompts 21 to 30

21. See what happens when you explore one of the following:

- My life as an aunt/uncle
- The worst mess I ever had to clean up
- Why I love ...
- If you want to annoy me, just ...

21. Think of all the meanings and expressions that relate to
the word "light." Here are some examples: light as a feather,
light bulb, light on her feet, light-headed, neon, incandescent,
bright, burnt out, light the way. Play with these until one of
them leads you to a story or poem.

22. Think of a sound that isn't around anymore: the click of
typewriter keys, the tone that played during the test pattern on
1950's TVs, the sound of the dial turning on a telephone, the
theme of an old TV or radio program, the sound of a former
pet's paws on hardwood floor, the sound of the doorbell of a
house you used to live in. What memories do those sounds con-
jure up? What rooms or people do you see?

23. Try one of these opening sentences:

- Tom had everything, except …
- If you couldn't arrange a solar eclipse to darken your day, there was always Henry.
- The winter wind rattled the windows.
- Dirt was fine—in its place.

24. How would you complete the following sentences? How would your characters complete the sentences?

- If I could be a kid again, I would …
- If I could go back to one day in my life, I would …
- If I could have one good-bye over again, I would …

25. What if—

- The antique bracelet found by your character was engraved with map coordinates and a date in the near future.
- A garden shed was really a time travel portal.
- A picnic basket held a wonderful romantic meal—and a gun.

26. Use one, some or all of these words in a story or poem: brush, mask, window, ring, fan.

27. What brings you comfort? A hug, the low vibration of a purring cat, fuzzy slippers and a favorite housecoat, ice cream, money in the bank, Jack Daniels? Explain why certain things

make you feel comforted. Now answer the same question for your character.

28. Write about a "body of water." Consider the following: a bubble bath, a puddle, a storm-blown lake, a calm green sea, a child's wading pool

29. Write a story using one of the following titles:

- White Night
- Murder and Shadow
- Spree for Two
- Dream Warrior

30. Try one of these opening sentences:

- He'd always had the perfect golf grip. The one he used on the gun wasn't bad either.
- Palm trees always reminded me of him/her.
- Parker was definitely not singing in the rain.
- I think that, after you lose your car keys three days in a row, you should just be able to stay home.

CHAPTER 5

Prompts 31 to 40

31. Use the following dialogue as a springboard to your story:

What do you mean you don't hear it?
Hear what?
Over there. Listen.
What am I supposed to be listening to?
You don't hear it?
No.
Then you'd better stay here.
Why?
Because I just heard my name.

32. Try one of these opening sentences:

- Pick up the sword.
- That is definitely not supposed to be lying on my front porch.
- Landlords must take special courses in how to be aggravating.

33. Use one, some or all of the following words in a story: bridge, note, match, string, dial

34. Write a story using one of the following titles:

- Yesterday's Coffee
- Keepsake
- The Art of Telling Lies
- One Small Step
- Party Time

35. Write about an incident involving a dog, a window, and a green hat from three points of view.

36. Have you ever wanted to get in your car or on a bus or train and just keep going? What is pulling you from where you are? What do you want to leave behind, if only for a while? What do you hope is ahead of you? What does your character think and do when he or she feels this way?

37. Use one, some or all of the following words in a story: circle, cliff, jewel, paper, snow, nail

38. Think about the meanings and expressions related to the word "glass." Here are some examples: glassy-eyed, glass half empty, glass of water/wine/..., eye glasses, smooth as glass, clear as glass, hourglass, magnifying glass, glass slippers ... Play with these until one of them leads you to a story or poem.

39. Try using one of these opening sentences:

- Only the desperate need apply.
- I'd had a lot of experience with death, but this time …
- If my smartphone was so smart why had it just called Jim?
- Sam shivered. It wasn't the cold.

40. Freewrite around the word "lonely." To what or whom do you turn when you are lonely? To what or whom does your character turn?

CHAPTER 6

Prompts 41 to 50

41. What makes your character stop and savor the moment? The peaty aroma of an Islay malt? A baby's smile? What special memory or feeling is evoked? How can this change of pace enhance your story and let the reader know your character better?

42. What has your character wasted in the past—money, time, a relationship, someone's trust? How does that event color what your character is doing today and how does it influence your character's choices? Answer the same question for yourself.

43. Think of things white. Choose one word to free write around and fill your white page with words: snow, teeth, clouds, wedding gowns, peonies and magnolias, paper, smoke, grubs ....

44. Free write around one, all, or some of the following words: ice, gift, map, moon, lamp.

45. Are you a lark? Describe your perfect morning. Are you an owl? Describe your perfect night?

46. Here are some more lines of dialogue. Have fun!

You're late. I thought you weren't going to make it.
I nearly didn't.
Do you have it with you?
Yes.
Good.
Can we go now?

47. Ask your character the ten Bernard Pivot questions that James Lipton asks his guests on the Actor's Studio. For fun, ask yourself, too!

- What is your favorite word?
- What is your least favorite word?
- What turns you on?
- What turns you off?
- What is your favorite curse word?
- What sound or noise do you love?
- What sound or noise do you hate?
- What profession other than your own would you like to attempt?
- What profession would you not like to do?
- If Heaven exists, what would you like to hear God say when you arrive at the Pearly Gates?

48. If you only had one window to look out of for the next six months, what would you want to see on the other side? Describe the view. How would it change? Why did you choose this particular view? Do the same exercise for your character? What did you learn?

49. What is your character's greatest fear? If your character doesn't have one, create one and make sure that he or she has to face that fear at a critical time in your story. Think Indiana Jones and the snakes.

50. What is the one 'good-bye' that you said to a living person that you regret saying? Answer the same question for your character.

.

CHAPTER 7

Prompts 51 to 60

51. Describe the best kiss you ever gave or received--or both.

52. Does your character prefer to be alone or with a lot of people? What benefits does your character derive from being in his favorite situation? How does he cope when he must experience the opposite? Think of placing your character in his least favorite setting and add another level of conflict to whatever else is happening in the scene.

53. Have you ever felt that you should have been born in a different decade? What draws you to this time? Write about what you would do on a typical day in your other decade.

54. What food do you hate? Consider serving your character her most despised meal in a situation where she feels she actually has to eat it.

55. Free write around one, some, or all of the following words: ring, storm, table, train, blue

56. Use these bare bones lines of dialogue to create a scene between two people. Add setting, character's thoughts and actions to fill in the gaps.

Are you ready?
Yes.
You're sure?
Yes.
You're not saying much.
There's no need.
You don't have to come.
I do. And you know it.

57. Choose one sentence from the opening paragraph of the novel you are currently reading and use it to begin your story. Here's mine from *The Tribune's Curse* by John Maddox Roberts: "If you are extremely happy, the gods have it in for you."

58. What place have you always wanted to visit? What attracts you to this place? What do you wish you could experience there? Answer these questions for your character.

59. What's your favorite film? What special quality does this film have that sets it apart from the rest? How can you add that special quality to your current writing project?

60. Many mystery novelists hook readers with their expertise in a certain skill: gourmet cooking, knitting, quilting, showing dogs. Do you have or know about a special skill that could add an extra dimension to your character?

CHAPTER 8

Prompts 61 to 70

61. Use these lines of dialogue to create a scene between two people. Add setting, character's thoughts and actions to fill in the gaps.

What are you doing?
What does it look like I'm doing?
Sorry. Forget it.
What do you want.
The book. It's on my list.
Help yourself, Bill

62. Think of veins. Think of them flowing with healthy blood, tracing delicate patterns in leaves, leaving cruel blue patterns on an old woman's legs, holding a rich deposit of gold, mutilated by drug use, taking in life-saving medication. Choose one vein of thought and write what you imagine.

63. If your main character could choose to play a character in a play or movie, which character would he or she choose? Which character would you choose?

64. Scour magazines and newspapers for interesting faces. Give them new names, professions and histories and see if they want to come and play in your story.

65. Freewrite around the following words: drink, call, space, ladder, jam, cliff.

66. Write a story for children. Start with "once upon a time" or "long ago in a land far away." Enjoy a magic place where anything can happen.

67. Several works share the title, "A Stitch in Time" derived from the saying: A stitch in time saves nine. What titles and stories can you create from other proverbs or sayings? Try one of these: What's good for the goose is good for the gander. Once bitten, twice shy. Where there's smoke, there's fire. Jack of all trades, master of none.

68. Write an opening paragraph in which your character comes into physical contact with someone or something.

69. Think about secrets. Make sure your character has some and imagine the kind of person he or she would trust with those secrets. How could that other person gain that trust? Why might that person betray that trust and tell the secret to someone else?

70. If you have an antique or flea market nearby, look for old postcards and read the messages on the back. Here's one I found. What story can you imagine lies behind this message? "I suppose you are still in Plaster Rock. Heard that Frank 1st has left you. I guess he must be a wanderer."

CHAPTER 9

Prompts 71 to 80

71. Brainstorm around the words: flame, table, cover, mask, hollow, leaf.

72. Send your characters on an adventure to a "land far, far away." Look through some old issues of *National Geographic* and imagine how your character would cope in a yurt, or in a market in Marrakesh or in a tent on the side of a mountain.

73. April showers bring May flowers. What flowers could you name your characters after? What kind of people do you associate with names such as Peony, Rose, Thorn, Lily? Here are some characters from stories you might know that are named after flowers: Molly Bloom, Flora Poste, Violet Beaudelaire, Scarlet Pimpernel, Fleur Forsyth, Fleur Delacour, Daisy Buchanan, Lily Owens, Violetta Valéry, Zinnia Larkin, and don't forget Scarlet O'Hara's original name was Pansy!

74. Begin your story with your character in motion—driving, running, flying, riding. What is your character running from? What is your character running to?

75. You're walking home with a friend after dark. When you look at her, her eyes reflect light like a cat's. What happens next?

76. Look at your favourite CD cover. Hide everything but one square inch. Describe what you see?

77. Free write around one or all of the following words: box, watch, garden, window, ship

78. Play with the word "needle." How many different needles can you visualize? Put one or two of them in your character's hands or just out of reach and see what happens. Here are some prompts: someone away from home for the first time sewing on a button, fearing a dentist's needle, needles clacking in Paris while heads roll... Or have your character be needled by someone or needle someone else.

79. Your character loses a backpack/ purse/briefcase containing one thing that his or her future depends upon. What happens next?

80. Write an opening sentence in which something or someone falls. What happens when they get up--or don't!

CHAPTER 10

Prompts 81 to 90

81. Turn off everything and try writing in silence or change your background sounds. Try jazz, blues, Benedictine monks, Mozart.

82. Think of the skills you have: putting up a tent, downhill skiing, solving crosswords, cooking. Add these skills and interests to your characters or make learning them essential for your main character's survival.

83. Use one of the following sentences to begin a story:

- White lace curtains fluttered in the warm breeze.
- The air was thick with wood smoke.
- I thought Play-Doh® was for kids until I saw the body
- Now I know what they really mean by "caught in the act."
- Erik loved the dark.
- Red warning lights flashed on the console.

84. Brainstorm around the word dry. Here are a few ideas to get you started--bone dry, dry out, dry as a desert, parched, dry dock.

85. Freewrite using one or all of the following words: sage, match, corner, light, border.

86. Elmore Leonard said, "I once named a character Frank Matisse, but he acted older than his age; and for some reason he wouldn't talk as much as I wanted him to. I changed his name to Jack Delany and couldn't shut him up." Try renaming one of your characters and see what happens.

87. Find a place where you can do some serious people-watching. Pick three strangers and, one by one, imagine them saying good-bye. Decide what they are saying good-bye to-- their homeland, their family, a lover, a job, a threat. What has happened to bring them to this moment? What lies ahead of them? Is the good-bye the beginning of their story or the end?

87. See where these lines of dialogue take you:

"Excuse me did you drop this?"
"No that's not mine."
"I think it is."

89. Start with the sound of sirens. How does that sound affect you? What do you imagine has happened? Where has it happened? Who is affected?

90. Use one of the following as a title for a story or poem:

• Rainbow Memory
• Yesterday's Rain

- Puddle Jumper
- Misty Morning
- Rain Delay

CHAPTER 11

Prompts 91 to 100

91. What does your character value the most? Is it an object like a ring or a photograph? Or is it a reputation for honesty or an influential position or the chance to find true love? How can you put what your character values most at serious risk in your story? What do you value most?

92. Use one, some or all of the following words to spark a story or poem: bloom, wall, flow, cup, eye, time

93. Use one of these opening sentences to start a story:

- Okay. Remind me again why I wanted to be a June bride.
- A black wall of cloud raced in from the west. Dead leaves scattered in the wind. Once again, the perfect setting for his arrival.
- I refused to let them see me cry.

94. June 21st marks the official beginning of summer. Use some of these summery titles and excerpts to frame a story, personal memory, or poem: A Summer Place, Summer in the City, Sunshine, Lollipops and Rainbows, The Summer Breeze, The Summer of '42, Summer

Wine, Shall I compare thee to a summer's day?, The Longest Day, Summer Holiday, Summer of '69.

95. See where these lines of dialogue take you:

"Come here and look at this!"
Kelly obediently peered over Mike's shoulder at the computer screen.
"What am I supposed to be looking at?"
"Linc's Twitter account's been hacked."
"Yeah, so? Happens to lots of people. The message usually says that someone is saying bad things about you and gives you a link you're supposed to be stupid enough to click on. No one falls for it anymore. Linc knows what to do."
"This message is different." Mike pointed at the screen. "Look."
Kelly read the message to herself and then again out loud. "They're going to kill me. Help."

96. Use one, some or all of the following words in a story or poem: shirt, pen, thunder, cry, case, paper.

97. Head to your local bookstore or library with a friend and your writing journal. Take two envelopes and lots of small pieces of paper. For five minutes wander the shelves and write random novel titles on the small pieces of paper and put them in your envelopes. At the end of five minutes, exchange envelopes. Dip in and pull out a title and brainstorm a story that would go with those words. Maybe you could use the words as a line of dialogue to begin your story or in the opening sentence. Keep playing until one story starts to claim your full attention. Start writing.

98. Draw a map. It could be of a country, a city, an island, a kingdom, a space station. Add lots of details and place names. Now send your characters on a journey through the imaginary world you have just created, making sure that they get into lots of trouble along the way.

99. Think of the places that you know well: a neighbourhood, a city, a school, a cruise ship, a gym, a museum, a summer camp. Now imagine them as places where your characters can fall in love or be shocked or frightened. They can be places where a murder takes place or where people reveal secrets.

100. I wish I may I wish I might have the wish I wish tonight. What wish would your character wish for upon a star or ask a genie to grant? What would be the consequences of that dream coming true? What would you wish for? Why? How would your life change if your wish came true?

CHAPTER 12

Prompts 101 to 110

101. Flowers don't just inspire people's names, but they inspire place names, too. What stories could you create in towns like these: Flower's Cove, Newfoundland; Strawberry, Arkansas; Weedpatch, California; Beanblossom, Indiana; Rosebud, Alberta; Carrot River, Saskatchewan; Olive Branch, Michigan; Fallen Leaf, California; Lady Slipper, Prince Edward Island; Tiger Lily, Saskatchewan.

102. Use one of the following sentences to begin a story:

- When I thought about the cabin, I only remembered the corners—the ones where I'd crouched in fear.
- I never dreamt it would be still standing after all these decades, but then, if my great aunt's diary was right, this simple weathered cabin was magic.
- I hated classical music, so fortunately for me the concert was cut short half way through the William Tell Overture—sadly so was the conductor's life.

103. Use some of these April-inspired song titles to inspire a story or poem.

> Crying in the Rain
> I'll Remember April
> Early Morning Rain
> April in Paris
> April Come She Will
> Rainy Days and Mondays

104. Try one of the following sentences to begin or end your story:

- Character 1: "Listen to the rain pounding on the roof!"//Character 2: "That's not rain."
- "Share my umbrella, lady?"
- "I thought you said this tent was waterproof!"
- After two hours of the brain-numbing, thud-swish of windshield wipers, Carol stopped her car.

105. Have your character find or receive something small enough to be held in two hands. Now create a story around that small thing that turns your character's life upside down. Think of Bilbo and a ring, Arthur and a sword, Snow White and an apple.

106. Use one or more of the following words in a story or poem: puddle, tree, letter, steps, trail, ache.

107. March 21st marks the vernal equinox when day and night hours are perfectly balanced. Do you strive for balance in

your life? How do you achieve it? How do you cope when the dark overwhelms the light in your life? How would your character answer these questions?

108.   Consider words/ideas associated with the words 'lion' and 'lamb' and see what stories are hiding in them: Lamb Chop, soft, woolly, Mary and the lamb, lamb to the slaughter, MGM's lion, roaring, fierce, Androcles and the Lion, Africa, Serengeti, pride, hunter, Lion King.

109.   Use one, some, or all of these words to spark a story or poem: march, crock, blue, bloom, roof, stone

110.   March has two astrological signs: Pisces the fish and Aries the ram. What characteristics are suggested by those two animals? Do they apply to anyone you know? Think about what animals your characters could be. When Laurence Olivier created his role of Richard III, he saw him as a spider.

CHAPTER 13

Prompts 111 to 120

111. Some opening sentences to play with.

- Marnie sat in front of her computer, staring at a screen full of photos. "Delete," she whispered and the screen went blank.
- A year had passed and it still hurt to walk in the house and not hear his voice.
- Pat walked into the library and flicked the light switch. A flash, a hollow pop, and darkness.

112. How does your main character accept a compliment? What is your main character a little (a lot) vain about?

113. Put an obstacle in your main character's way by changing the weather. Introduce some high winds into the story. Stop an escape with a fallen tree. Blow sand into his eyes. Have the rain make so much noise she can't sleep. Signal a weather change and send him down with a migraine.

114. Think about the different forms of power: personal, financial, political, power of nature, power of the weak, super-power, electrical, etc. What power is in the hands of the

antagonist or your main character's family, friends, lover that make your main character's task even harder? What power does your main character exert on others?

115. Brainstorm or free write around one or all of the following words: glass, willow, tile, edge, hollow, bar.

116. What stories would you write for these titles? In Cold Blood, Twice Shy, The Winter Sea, Cat Among the Pigeons, The Most Dangerous Game, The Sound of Thunder

117. Think of the most bizarre item that could be delivered by courier. Write about the recipient. Write about the sender.

118. Write a letter to yourself to be opened ten/twenty years from now. What do you want that person in the future to know or remember about you now? What do you want that person to have accomplished? Try the same exercise for your character.

119. Write a poem/story from the point of view of: an alarm clock, a road map, a baseball cap.

120. You're the family photographer in a large department store. Imagine a family that has come to have their photograph taken for a holiday card. What do you see that the family doesn't see or that the family doesn't want you to see?

CHAPTER 14

Prompts 121 to 130

121. You're on a bus and you don't know anyone. 1) You people watch. What do you see? OR 2) Not knowing anyone suddenly scares you. What happens next?

122. Use one, some or all of these words in a story or poem: empty, bowl, crack, window, yellow.

123. Try one of these opening sentences:

- Okay. Fine. I'll do it.
- If you're hungry, you'll eat it.
- The next time I say 'yes' I'm actually going to listen to the question.
- I thought this was supposed to be a vacation.

124. Write about pain. It can be physical or emotional or both.

125. Write a story using one of the following titles:

- The Talisman
- Mister Murder

- Elephants Never Forget
- A Kind of Peace
- Among the Lost

126. How concerned is your character about global warming and conservation? Does he or she recycle or have a garden or compost or drive a hybrid? How does this concern or lack of it affect day-to-day decisions and choices that your character makes?

127. Use the following dialogue as a springboard to a story:

I think we're going in the wrong direction.
What did you say?
I said, I think we're going in the wrong direction.
You just might be right.

128. Think of a time when you made a difficult choice. Remember how it felt and how you carried on afterwards. Think about the motives behind your decision. Now imagine that you are the kind of person who would have chosen to do the very opposite. Write from this person's point of view describing his or her motivations, feelings, and how the consequences were dealt with.

129. Take a risk—at least in imagination. Take the bungee jump, extreme ski, sing in front of thousands, and then write about it. Make sure that you use all your senses to describe your adventure.

130. If you could take back any words that you said, what would they be? Why would you want to take them back? What words would you character choose? Why?

CHAPTER 15

Prompts 131 to 140

131. Try using one of these opening sentences:

- The sign says, "No Trespassing."
- In a perfect world chocolate would be calorie free.
- Heartbeats shouldn't be this loud.
- Mike heard the click and froze.

132. Use the following dialogue as a springboard to your story:

There's a storm coming.
Soon?
We have about an hour.
That should be long enough.

133. Use one, some or all of the following words in a story: pane, river, stone, open, branch, cloud.

134. Use the word "house" to search for images on the internet. Choose a house that appeals to you and imagine a family that lives there and what their story might be. What do they see

when they look out their windows? What's in the basement? Or the attic?

135. Write about an incident involving a door, a stain, and a sigh from three points of view.

136. Freewrite around the word "empty." A few prompts: An empty nest can be a lonely place or a new freedom. An empty journal can be an opportunity to create. An empty bottle …

137. Describe a moment when you were surprised. Did the surprise make you happy or sad or frightened? Describe a similar moment for your character.

138. Write a story using one of the following titles:

- A Fine Romance
- Dead at Dinner
- Whispers
- The Dragon's Curse

139. Is your character a planner or is your character spontaneous? Is he or she happy when someone just drops by or only happy when visits are planned and prepared for?

140. Have some fun with words relating to time. Here are few to get you started: Big Ben, stopwatch, time passes, time limit, running out of time, race against time, Time Lord, timeless.

CHAPTER 16

Prompts 141 to 150

141. What would be your perfect vacation destination? Who would be your ideal travel companions? What would you do there? How would you feel if you never had to come home? Answer these questions for your story's main character, too.

142. See what happens when you brainstorm around the word "sand." Here are a few suggestions to get you started— hour glass, sand trap, sand between your toes, dunes.

143. Some opening sentences for you to try:

- Fences are for climbing.
- Who says you never forget how to ride a bike.
- The rain and the mud were bad enough; I didn't need her smirk, too.
- Alex threw the sack onto the table.

144. See if one of these titles sparks a story or poem: Far From Love, The Lucas Curse, By Common Consent, Honor Among Thieves.

145. Look at your favorite magazine. Look carefully at the faces and people in the magazine until you find one that connects with you. Create a history for that person. Tell his or her story.

146. Use one, some or all of the following words to create a story, poem or scene: cap, link, wheel, funnel, pot, turret.

147. How many times a day do you check your watch or phone for the time? Are you checking to see how much time has passed or how much is left? Do you manage time well or do things just get done when they get done? How do your story's characters feel about the passage of time?

148. Have you ever felt that you have 'burned your bridges' with a friend, family member, or employer? What happened? Has this happened to your character? What happened to him or her? How can this cause a complication in the story you are writing?

149. Some opening sentences for you to try:

- Just a few more steps
- Only three days to save his life.
- Even though the umbrella cast a wide shadow, I still wondered if dead skin could sunburn.
- The candle guttered and we were left in the dark.

150. Use one, some or all of the following words to create a story, poem or scene: glasses, stake, pool, shadow, crest, choke.

CHAPTER 17

Prompts 151 to 160

151. How do you communicate with those you love? Do you call, or Skype, or text? Is it important to hear their voices or see their faces? Are words enough? How do your characters keep in touch? Is there anything they miss as they keep in touch?

152. Use one, some or all of the following words to create a story, poem or scene: bricks, crack, stain, twine, reach, pry.

153. Some opening sentences for you to try:

- Dad's tree was dying.
- His watch has stopped.
- Feet scrabbled into the shadows.
- Only the body disturbed the smooth surface of the pool.

154. Try the word "seat" as a starting place for some free-writing. Here are a few suggestions: throne, kitchen chair, chaise lounge, subway, lawn chair.

155. How much do you know about your family? Does any-one ever compare you to one of your relatives? How do you feel about the comparison? Do you speculate that other family mem-

bers that you don't know might be like you? How do your characters relate to their relatives?

156. When did you last see your best friend? Describe what you did and what you talked about. Why is this person so special to you? Answer the same questions for your character.

157. How have you felt when you faced a "significant" birthday? What thoughts when through your mind? What resolutions did you make for the next year, the next decade? Is age just a number for you? How does your character feel about his or her age or upcoming birthday?

158. Use the word "fly" to spark your imagination. Here are a few ideas: dragonfly, no fly zone, jet, insect, soar, "Come Fly With Me."

159. Some opening sentences for you to try:

- Put that down.
- Dear Diary.
- I didn't expect to be happy he was dead.
- This was absolutely the wrong time for the fuse to blow.

160. When is the last time you cried? Describe what happened. Describe what happened the last time your character cried.

CHAPTER 18

Prompts 161 to 170

161. What do you do/feel when you find out that you've been lied to? How does your character react?

162. Try the word "step" to create a scene or a story. Here are a few connections to start: step ladder, step aside, step to the back, watch your step, out of step, step-mother.

163. See if one of these titles sparks a story or poem: The Red Roof, Dog Days, Winters Are Murder, Paper Lies.

164. How do you cope when you get a cold? Head for bed or work through it or ...? How does your character deal with being sick?

165. Who is your favorite author in the genre you write in? Have you researched his or her life? What is your favorite book? What writing lessons can you take away from your favorites?

166. Use one, some or all of the following words to create a story, poem or scene: lake, call, face, track, grind, shelter, breath.

167.   What's your favorite cartoon strip in the newspapers? Why does it appeal to you? Which comic strip is a must-read for your character? Why?

168. See what happens when you play with these lines of dialogue:

I think you need to reconsider.
Why?
Look behind you.
Oh.

169.   Think of what you can create using with the word "snap." Here are a few places you can start: card game, twig, snapdragon, snap of the fingers, turtle.

170. What represents stability to you? Do you value stability in your life or do you prefer to live with a lot of uncertainty? Why do you think you feel this way? Answer these questions for your character?

CHAPTER 19

Prompts 171 to 180

171. See if one of these titles sparks a story or poem: The Lady Takes A Bite, Catch, Guardian's Promise, Cat's Lament.

172. Do you prefer silence or noise when you work? Why? Answer the same questions for your character.

173. See where the word "ball" can take your imagination: Here are a few prompts: Cinderella, basket, bearing, beach, ball and chain.

174. If your story were going to be filmed, who would star? Why would they be the best match for your characters?

175. Some opening sentences for you to try:

- If I heard that whistle one more time …
- His hand trembled as he closed the book.
- The creature slipped into the long grass.
- Only animals' eyes are supposed to glow at night.

176. Who is your favorite superhero or folk hero? Why is this person so compelling? Which super/folk hero is your character's favorite? Why?

177. What topic does someone have to introduce into a conversation for you to shut down? What topic do you never want to talk about? What topic causes this reaction in your character? Why?

178. What would be your favorite place to go for a walk? What would your five senses experience there? How does being in this place make you feel? Answer these questions for your character.

179. See if one of these titles sparks a story or poem: Pool Party, The Deadly Season, Hard Drive, Broken Glass.

180. Use one, some or all of the following words to create a story, poem or scene: bird, scrape, clock, envy, whistle, sunset.

CHAPTER 20

Prompts 181 to 190

181. How do you feel when you are doing something that you don't want to do, or are spending time with people you don't like? How do you cope? How does your character feel in these situations?

182. Play with the word "black" and see what story or poem ideas turn up. Here are a few ideas to get you started: licorice, cat, magic, widow, knight.

183. Here are some lines of dialogue. Can you think of characters and a setting that make these lines work?

I'm not going in there.
What's the problem?
It's dark and it stinks.
And?
Okay, I'm going in there.

184. Use one, some or all of the following words to create a story, poem or scene: border, willow, rust, wine, fortune, still.

185. If you could instantly fix anything in your life right now, what would it be? Would you change anything or have trouble picking just one thing? What would your character want to fix—nor not?

186. Here are some story titles. See what stories you can imagine to go with them: Today and Tomorrow, Luke's Journey, Face in the Mirror, One More Mile.

187. Try one of these opening sentences to start a story:

- I didn't need to smell the place to know why I hated it.
- Please tell us a little about yourself.
- Haven't you ever seen a knife before?
- It will be here any minute.

188. What strategies do you use to comfort a friend who is going through a bad time? What advice do you give or what do you say to help this person feel better? Is this something your character is good at, or does he or she try to avoid these moments as much as possible?

189. Describe in detail what is in your character's pockets or purse or backpack. Why does your character carry these things with him or her all the time?

190. What kind of driver are you? How do you feel about your car? Is it just a simple necessity or does it say a lot about who you are? Answer these questions for your character.

CHAPTER 21

Prompts 191 to 201

191. What's your favorite board or card game? Why do you enjoy it? Who are your favorite gaming partners? How competitive are you? Do you enjoy the game whether you win or lose? Answer these questions for your character.

192. Try these lines of dialogue and see where they take you.

I have to talk to you.
Why should I listen.
Because this time I'm not lying.

193. Can you think of a story for these titles? Packed Bags, One Shoe Missing, Book Club, Just a Short Walk.

194. Use one, some or all of these words in a story or poem: fan, wrong, shot, games, cord, note, window.

195. What would you do with a large inheritance? What would your character do if he or she inherited a large sum of money?

196. Here's the last set of story titles for you to play with. Wonder Mountain, Mended Fences, Brett's Cabin, Getting Charlie.

197. Here's the last set of lines of dialogue for you.

What's that in your hand?
Nothing.
It's not "nothing." Your hand is red.

198. Here's your last set of opening sentences:

- Sit down, or else.
- The wind was changing. I felt it in my skin.
- Never lend Parker anything.
- The sound of his voice never failed to make me cringe.

199. If someone asked you to describe one happy moment from your childhood, what would it be? Would you have trouble choosing only one? Or would you have difficulty finding any to choose from? How would your character answer this question?

200. Think about fences. What do they keep in? What do they keep out? What happens when the fence breaks?

201. How important is it for you to be a writer? What strategies do you use to make sure that you have time to write and follow your writing dreams? If you have trouble finding the time or inspiration, please read the following chapter excerpted from *Writing Fiction: A Hands-On Guide for Teens*. I hope you find

all the time you need to be creative and that all your writing dreams come true.

Keeping the Writer in You Motivated

Here are eight tricks, thoughts, and suggestions for keeping your writer in creative gear when the demands of the rest of your life try to make that impossible.

Rethink what you really need to be a writer.

At the most basic level you need a pencil and paper and the will to apply one to the other for a period of time. You don't need a computer to write the first draft of anything. If you need it, then you have to be in the same room with it. And that means you can't write anywhere else or in any other way. Think about how limiting that is. When time to write is so scarce, limiting yourself to one writing location can make it nearly impossible to write at all.

Promise yourself writing time and make a space for it in your life every day.

This can be a difficult promise to keep but it can be done. Consider setting the alarm for an earlier time and hitting the page before the rest of your day begins to crowd in. Dorothea

Brande, author of *Becoming a Writer* recommends a half-hour of writing in the morning right after you wake up and before you talk to anyone or even read. "…[What] you are actually doing is training yourself, in the twilight zone between sleep and the full waking state, simply to write." Like any muscle, the writing one needs regular exercise, too.

Give yourself a twenty-minute gift of writing time.

Don't tell yourself that there's no point in starting because you don't have a clear three hours to write. Inspiration will find you if you're on the bus, waiting for the movie to start, or the dentist to call you in. If you're meeting a friend for coffee, get there twenty minutes early and take your notebook. Those twenty-minute blocks add up, and think about it, writing for twenty minutes is better than not writing at all.

Set a goal.

Perhaps you decide that you want to write 2,000 words in a week. If you're a natural born procrastinator, you might need to break your goal down into small daily chunks. Remember to be easy on yourself if you don't make every personal writing deadline. One chocolate bar doesn't end a diet. You have a lot in your life right now. Congratulate yourself on what you did do, because each page you filled got you closer to your goal. And there's always another day, or another twenty-minute gift that you can give to yourself.

Never stop thinking of yourself as a writer.

When you wake up, think about what you will do for the writer today. Eavesdrop on a conversation and record one really good line? Read great writing? Write down three unrelated words and think of a story that will connect them? Add a paragraph to your current piece? Do some research? Edit a page? Buy a new pencil? Use the word 'writer' to define yourself and you will honor your commitment to the writer as you do to the friend, spouse, child, parent, sibling, boss, and co-worker who also need your attention every day.

Lose the perfectionist.

Give yourself permission to write a first draft that is a mess. Just get the words down. They don't have to be the words that end up in the final story. That's what second drafts--and thirds-- are for. Anne Lammot, author of *Bird by Bird*, says, "The first draft is the child's draft, where you let it all pour out and then let it romp allover the place, knowing that no one is going to see it and that you can shape it later." If Anne Lammot's advice doesn't connect to you, consider Miss Frizzle's: "Take chances, make mistakes, and get messy!"

Have more than one story or poem on the go.

That way, you will always have something to write, even if one idea is dead or your inspiration for it is. Remember, too, that you don't have to write a story or a poem in order. If you have a clear idea of how a scene or description or a stanza will work later on, write it now and connect it later. But write.

The best advice is last: Start now!

Final Words

INSPIRATION – BE READY FOR IT!

INSPIRATION: Stimulus to do creative work; something that stimulates the human mind to creative thought or to the making of art. Encarta Dictionary

Things come along every day that inspire, that are great ideas for stories or novels or poems. But creativity needs more than inspiration. What do you need, as the definition says, to make the art? The first step you need to take is to be a working writer. And working writers do more than pound keyboards all day. When you're out in the world are you open to new sights and sounds? Do you take a moment to look at the sunset or sunrise, or listen to the sounds of your neighborhood—radios, leaf blowers, dogs barking, airplanes, trucks, road construction, a motorcycle a few blocks away. Where else are you going to get the vivid details that will paint the picture that your inspiration suggests?

Do you listen to people? Not just to your own circle of friends and family, but to people on the bus or at work? What are their speech rhythms and patterns like? Do their voices go up at the end of sentences? Perhaps, they use a lot of technical jargon, or catch phrases like 'you know' or 'it's like' or 'so.' Do they talk about their kids all the time or complain about the boss? All of these details make up the palette from which you create your word pictures—your stories and poems.

At a workshop I attended recently, I heard from a woman who had lots of story ideas. She shared some with us, and they were wonderful. She was definitely inspired and clearly had the tools to create wonderful pictures for her listeners. She was also a self-confessed procrastinator. What a shame. She wanted to be a writer so much but had never made her dream come true, because she kept putting it off.

Do you keep saying that you'll write that story or novel 'someday'? Make that someday now. Many NaNoWriMo writers have gone through the exercise of finding the time to write a novel in a month. Log your activities, hour by hour, for a week. Find out where you can take the time to get your writing done. Do you need to watch all those TV shows when they're on? Can you record them and watch them some other time? Having a big chunk of time for writing is wonderful, but it can be very intimidating to fill with constructive work especially if you're not used to it. Chipping away at a project a little at a time is a great solution and also helps you develop the habit of sitting at the keyboard, or somewhere with pencil and paper, and writing every day.

Make sure you keep reading, too. Immerse yourself in someone else's writing. Read the words aloud to hear the rhythms and understand how the author keeps the action moving with sentence variety. Expand your vocabulary. Look up words the author uses that you don't know. When you are writing your story and looking for just the right word, you'll have it at your fingertips. Vary your reading so that you read in different genres and forms: mystery, sci-fi, literary, romance, poetry, adventure, short stories. When inspiration strikes, you can take your ideas and frame them in the form and style of writing that serves them best.

Lastly, write even when you're not inspired. Athletes practise when it's not race day and writers need to write even when there's no deadline or no real inspiration. Writing "muscles" need to be kept in trim, too. Finding words and putting them together with depth of meaning and in a way that grabs a reader needs to be a daily habit not just an intermittent exercise that you take on when the mood strikes you.

You don't need to write for a long time, even a little bit will make a difference to how you feel about facing the page the next day. Keeping a daily journal is one way to strengthen those muscles and keep them flexed. Another is to play with words whenever you can. Take a page from the novel you are reading, point to three random words on a page, and see what you can make from them. Take a line from a song you like and use that to start a story or a poem. Describe what you see out of your window, or write from a different point of view, such as that of your baseball cap, or your backpack, or your running shoes, or your alarm clock. Who knows? You may be inspired. And when you are, you'll have all the tools you need to create your work of art.

I wish you every success and lots of fun with your writing!

****

If you have time, I'd appreciate an honest review of the book at your favourite online bookseller. Your words are appreciated and they matter.

ABOUT THE AUTHOR

Heather Wright is a busy freelancer, children's writer and part-time professor. As a freelancer, Heather has worked for educational publishers, non-profits and agencies. Her feature articles, profiles and promotional copy have appeared in local and national publications.

She loves research and has enjoyed writing many stories with historical settings for *Kayak: Canada's History Magazine for Kids.* Her books for middle readers and teens include *Sherlock Holmes and the Orphanage Mystery, Writing Fiction: A Hands-On Guide for Teens, Writing Fiction: A Guide for Pre-Teens, The Dragon's Pearl,* and *The Dragon's Revenge,* all available at on-line bookstores.

Heather enjoys working with young writers and loves to visit classrooms to teach writing skills and to talk about various aspects of the writer's life. She runs teen writing workshops at her local library and at art camps, and has also created presentations for conferences and the public.

Her website, **http://wrightingwords.com,** hosts her blog and lots of resources for teen and pre-teen writers and their teachers.

www.ingramcontent.com/pod-product-compliance
Lightning Source LLC
Chambersburg PA
CBHW06020820290526
45789CB00003B/1214